MISS BRAIN'S

Cool Math Games

FOR KIDS IN GRADES 3-5

by Kelli Pearson

Copyright © 2012, 2016, 2019 by Kelli Pearson. All rights reserved.

Limited Reproduction Permission: The owner of this book may copy or otherwise reproduce parts of this book for personal or single classroom use.

Except as noted above, no part of this publication may be reproduced, stored in a retrieval system, or transmitted by any means—electronic, mechanical, or otherwise—without the prior written permission of the publisher. The use of this book with an entire school or district or for commercial use is strictly prohibited.

Artful Math
P.O. Box 3137
Santa Clara, CA 95055
http://www.artfulmath.com

First Revised Edition

Acknowledgements & Credits:
Heart, spade, club, diamond icons made by Freepik.com from www.flaticon.com
Coins stack icon by Ben Davis from the Noun Project
Bean icon by Pavitra from the Noun Project
Chat box icon by vectlab from the Noun Project
Paper Clip icon by Mike Rowe from the Noun Project

For my mom.

I love you forever.

table of contents

INTRODUCTION...1
Stuff You Will Need 2
How To Learn With Games 3

1. NUMBER SENSE GAMES.......................................4
Numbaroll 6
Sneaky 15 7
Likeable Numbers 8
Garbage Dump 9
Secret Number 10
Rounding X's 11
Add 'Em Up..12

2. ADDITION & SUBTRACTION GAMES................14
Cross Out Singles 16
Clear the Deck 17
Skunk 18
Penny Nickel Dime 19
Ninety Nine 20
Farkle Junior 22
Close to Zero 23
999 to Zero 24

3. MULTIPLICATION & DIVISION GAMES.............26
Lucky Numbers 28
Clippy 29
Just the Facts 30
Two Thousand 31

iv

Factors & Multiples 32
Remainder of Zero 33
2-3-5 34
Super Six 35
Buzz 36

4. FRACTION & DECIMAL GAMES.................38

Snacktions 40
Copy Cat 41
Fracto Giganto 42
Pizza! 43
The Betting Game 44
Zombies 46
Get in Line 48
Round Four 49

5. MIXED SKILL GAMES..............................50

Bowling for Numbers 52
Flip It 53
Algebra Balance Game 54
Bounce 55
Four Strikes & You're Out 56
Best Bingo Game Ever 58

PRINTABLE PAGES......................................60

Hundred Chart 62
Rounding X's Game Board 63
Add 'Em Up Score Card 64
Cross Out Singles Game Board 65
Clear the Deck Game Board 66
Skunk Game Board 67
Penny Nickel Dime Game Board 68

Clippy Game Board 69
2-3-5 Game Board 70
Fraction Strips 71
Pizza Game Board 72
Get in Line Game Board 73
Round Four Game Board 74
Bowling for Numbers Game Board 75
Algebra Balance Score Sheet 76
Bingo Game Board 77

MATH DICTIONARY 79

INDEX 86

introduction

Stuff You Will Need 2

How to Learn With Games 3

stuff you will need

You can play almost all of the games in this book with just a few basic supplies:

1. DICE
2. COINS*
3. DECK OF CARDS
4. PRINTABLES**

*You'll need 50 pennies, 20 nickels, 30 dimes and 10 quarters for the money games. Keep coins in a special jar for math games.

**All the printables in the back of the book can be downloaded online at

artfulmath.com/miss-brain-extras

You'll also find links to buy dice, cards, and other goodies.

how to learn with games

Did you know **games can help you learn?**

Here are some ways playing games helps you learn math:

- Games **relax you.**
- Games **make math fun**.
- Games **make math make sense**.
- You **remember more** when you're playing and active.
- The more you play these games, the **better you get at math!**

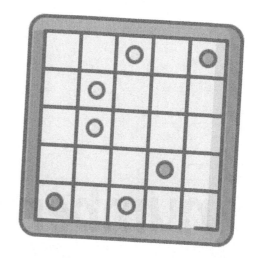

Math games are so much fun that you might even think, "This isn't math!" But you're actually learning a lot when you play.

A good game should feel not too easy, and not too hard.

If it's too hard, wait a few months then try that game again. If it's too easy, play the LEVEL UP! version at the bottom of the page.

LEVEL UP! is a more challenging way to play the game that will make it more fun for you as you get better at math.

number sense games

Numbaroll 6

Sneaky 15 7

Likeable Numbers 8

Garbage Dump 9

Secret Number 10

Rounding X's 11

Add 'Em Up 12

About how many jelly beans do you think are in this jar?

If you had three identical jars of jelly beans, about how many would that be?

You can make good guesses about numbers because you have **number sense**.

Number sense is your idea of how numbers work in real life. The more you count, estimate, and play with numbers, the better you'll get at number sense.

Real-life math like measuring, counting money, and cooking with a recipe are also great ways to get better at number sense.

Play the games in this chapter to get better at estimating and rounding, reading and writing big numbers, and digging deeper into how numbers work.

numbaroll

PLAYERS: 2
SKILL: place value, reading big numbers
YOU NEED: deck of cards, dice

1. Take out the face cards (jack, queen, king) and tens. Put the deck face down on the table.

2. Roll two dice.

3. Take that many cards. Lay them out on the table to make a large number

4. If you roll a 1, put down one card and roll again. Take more cards and add them to your number.

I rolled a 5, so I made a number with 5 cards: 97,541

5. Use your die as a comma in your number. Read the number out loud. The other player writes your score as you read it.

6. Play until all the cards are used up. Add your scores. Highest score wins.

sneaky 15

PLAYERS: 2
SKILL: odd/even, addition, logic
YOU NEED: paper & pencil

1. Draw a 3x3 tic tac toe grid.

2. The goal is to get three numbers in a row that add up to 15.

3. Choose one player to be Odd and another player to be Even. Odd goes first.

4. Take turns writing a number in the grid. Odd can write 1, 3, 5, 7 or 9. Even can write 2, 4, 6 or 8.

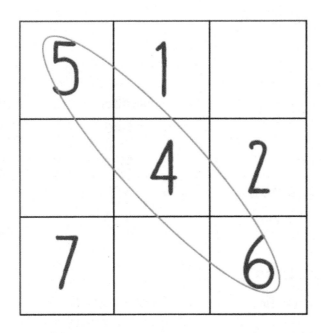

5. The first player to get three numbers in a row that add to 15 is the winner.

likeable numbers

PLAYERS: 2 or more
SKILL: reasoning, logic
YOU NEED: paper & pencil

1. Draw a line down the middle of your paper. On one side, write "Numbers I Like". On the other side write, "Numbers I Don't Like."

2. The numbers you like follow a secret rule. Don't tell the other player your rule. Your secret rule might be:

    * Odd numbers
    * Numbers that have an 8
    * Numbers that are all straight lines (like 14)
    * Numbers you can count to by 5s

3. The other players take turns guessing a number from 1 to 100.

4. If the number follows your rule, write it under "Numbers I Like". If not, write it under "Numbers I Don't Like".

5. Players can test as many numbers as they like, but they will have only two chances to guess your rule.

6. If they can't guess the rule in 2 tries, you win.

Numbers I Like	Numbers I Don't Like
10	27
90	4
35	38

My secret rule is multiples of 5

garbage dump

PLAYERS: 2-4
SKILL: place value, reading numbers
YOU NEED: paper & pencil, one die

1. The goal of Garbage Dump is to make the largest number you can.

2. Make 4 lines and a box on your paper like this:

   __ __ __ __ ☐

3. Roll the die.

4. Write the number you rolled on one of the lines. This is a digit in your number.

5. If you roll a low number, write it in the box. This is the garbage dump and is not part of your number.

6. You may not move a number once you write it.

7. When all the spaces are filled in, read your number out loud. The player with the highest number wins.

level up!

Draw more lines to make a bigger number.

__ __ __ , __ __ __ , __ __ __ ☐

secret number

PLAYERS: 2 or more
SKILL: number sense
YOU NEED: paper & pencil

1. Think of a 2-digit number. Don't say it out loud.

2. Other players will try to guess your number. Write all the guesses in a list on a piece of paper.

3. Draw circles next to each number as clues:

    ○ EMPTY CIRCLE: right digit in the wrong place

    ● FILLED IN CIRCLE: right digit in the right place

4. For example, let's say my secret number is 29. Here are kids' guesses and the clues that go with them:

62	○	There is a 2, but it's in the wrong place.
24	●	Now there is one right digit in the right place.
29	●●	Two filled in circles: both digits in the right place.

5. Play until someone guesses your number.

level up!

Play with a 3-digit number.

rounding x's

PLAYERS: 2-4
SKILL: number sense
YOU NEED: Rounding X's Game Board, deck of cards

1. Print or copy the Rounding X's Game Board.

2. Remove the 10s, jacks, queens, kings, and jokers from the deck. Leave in the aces (aces equal 1).

3. Put the cards in a pile face down on the table.

4. Draw two cards. Make a 2-digit number with the cards.

5. Round the number to the nearest tens place.

6. Put an X in the box with the rounded number.

7. For example: Your cards are 2 and 6. You make the number 62 and round it to 60. Put an X in the 60 box.

8. The first player with three X's in one box wins.

level up!

The first player with an X in every box wins.

add 'em up

PLAYERS: 1-2
SKILL: number sense, addition, mental math
YOU NEED: dice, Add 'Em Up Score Card

1. Print a copy of the Add 'Em Up Score Card.

2. Roll 2 dice. Write the number in the "hundreds" column.

3. Roll 2 dice a second time. Write the number in the "tens" column.

4. Roll 2 dice one more time. Write the number in the "ones" column.

5. Add the totals and write your score for each round.

6. Play 5 rounds. Who got the highest score?

hundreds		tens		ones		score
6	+	4	+	7	=	647
2	+	11	+	8	=	318
	+		+		=	

addition & subtraction games

Cross Out Singles..16

Clear the Deck 17

Skunk 18

Penny Nickel Dime 19

Ninety Nine 20

Farkle Junior 22

Close to Zero 23

999 to Zero 24

Addition and subtraction are everywhere.

Let's say you're at the store, checking out one of your favorite toys.

Can you afford it?

You check your pockets and add up your money. You subtract the price of the toy.

...And YES, you have enough money to buy it!

In real life, you will do a lot of **addition and subtraction in your head**. This chapter will help you get better at that.

Mental math can be tricky at first, but it gets easier the more you do it.

Play these fun games to keep your skills sharp and get better at mental math.

cross out singles

PLAYERS: 2-6
SKILL: addition, logic
YOU NEED: Cross Out Singles Game Board, dice

1. Roll one die. Write the number in one of the boxes.

2. Take turns rolling and writing in numbers until all nine boxes are filled in.

3. Add the numbers in each row, column, and diagonal. Write the total in the circle that comes after it.

4. Cross out any numbers that don't have a match in another circle.

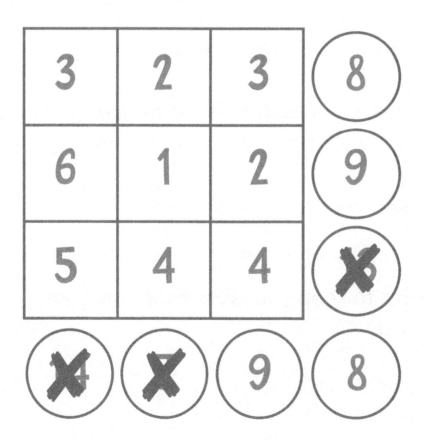

5. Add the numbers in the circles that are not crossed out.

6. Play 5 rounds and add all your scores.

clear the deck

PLAYERS: 2-4
SKILL: addition, probability
YOU NEED: Clear the Deck Game Board, rocks, dice

1. Print or draw a Clear the Deck Game Board for each player.

2. Put 8 rocks (or other small objects) on the game board. It's ok to put more than one rock on the same number.

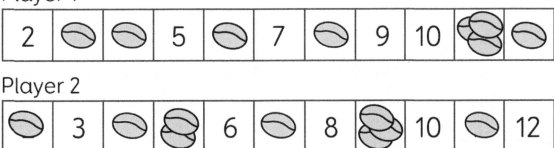

3. Roll 2 dice and add them together.

4. Take one rock off of that number.

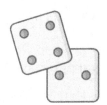

5. Take turns rolling and removing rocks.

6. If you roll a number that does not have a rock, skip your turn.

7. The first player to get rid of all their rocks wins.

level up!

Which numbers get rolled the most? What strategy can you use to set up your board so you can get rid of your rocks the fastest?

skunk

PLAYERS: 2 and up
SKILL: addition, probability
YOU NEED: Skunk Game Board, dice

1. Print or draw a Skunk Game Board for each player.

S	K	U	N	K
6				
10				
5				

2. All players stand up.

3. Roll 2 dice. Add them together. All players write this score in the S column.

4. You can keep standing and keep rolling to add to your S score. But be careful...if someone rolls a 1, the players who are standing lose all their points in that column.

5. Decide on each roll whether you want to stand and try to add to your points, or sit and keep the points you've got.

6. If someone rolls two 1's while you are standing, you lose ALL your points so far!

7. When everyone is sitting (or loses all their points), move on to the next letter. Everyone must stand for the first roll of a letter.

8. Add your points. The player with the most points wins.

penny nickel dime

PLAYERS: 2-6
SKILL: addition, counting money, logic
YOU NEED: Penny Nickel Dime Game Board, dice

1. Print a Penny Nickel Dime Game Board for each player, or draw your own.

2. Roll two dice. Let's say you roll a 4 and a 2.

3. Each player decides whether to take that many pennies, that many nickels, or that many dimes.

4. Fill in your game board for that roll.

5. You will roll 7 times, and add money each time.

6. The player who gets closest to $1.00 after 7 rolls without going over wins.

	Number Rolled	Penny, Nickel or Dime?	Money This Turn	Money So Far
1	5	dimes	.50	.50
2	6	nickels	.30	.80
3				
4				

ninety nine

PLAYERS: 2-6
SKILL: addition, mental math
YOU NEED: deck of cards, rocks or pennies

1. Aces are 1 or 11. Jack, queen and king are worth 10.

2. Give each player 3 cards. Put the rest of the deck face down on the table.

3. Play a card face up on the table. Say the number.

4. Take a new card after each turn so you always have 3 cards in your hand.

5. The next player plays a card on top of yours and adds to the total.

EXAMPLE: If the last card was a 2 and you play a 5, say "seven"

6. If you play a card that brings the total past 99, you lose a life.

ninety nine

7. When you are getting close to 99, there are some special cards to keep you in the game...

SPECIAL CARDS AND TRICKS

3 = add zero

4 = add zero and reverse direction

10 = minus 10 points

9 = go straight to 99

play the same card on top of another = add zero

8. Keep playing until there is just one player left. All the other players lose a life. That person wins the round.

farkle junior

PLAYERS: 2-4
SKILL: addition
YOU NEED: paper & pencil, 6 dice

1. Roll 6 dice and look for ways to get points:

    ❋ Each 5 is 50 points
    ❋ Each 1 is 100 points
    ❋ Three 1's is 300 points
    ❋ Three 2's is 200 points
    ❋ Three 3's is 300 points
    ❋ Three 4's is 400 points
    ❋ Three 5's is 500 points
    ❋ Three 6's is 600 points
    ❋ Four of the same number is 1,000 points
    ❋ 1, 2, 3, 4, 5, 6 is 1,000 points

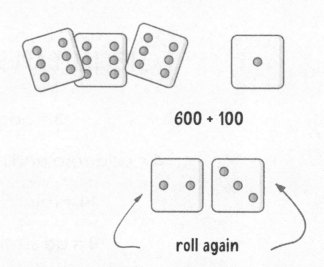

600 + 100

roll again

2. Add your points. Write your score so far and take out any dice that make points.

3. You can keep rolling with the leftover dice to try and get more points, or you can stop.

4. If you get more points, add them to your total.

5. **Careful:** If you roll and get no points, you lose ALL your points for that round!

6. Add up your total for the round.

7. Play 5 rounds. The person with the most points wins.

close to zero

PLAYERS: 2-6
SKILL: subtraction, number sense, logic
YOU NEED: paper & pencil, cards

1. Take out the 10s, jacks, queens and kings. Aces =1.

2. Deal 4 cards to each player.

3. Make an equation to subtract two 2-digit numbers, like this:

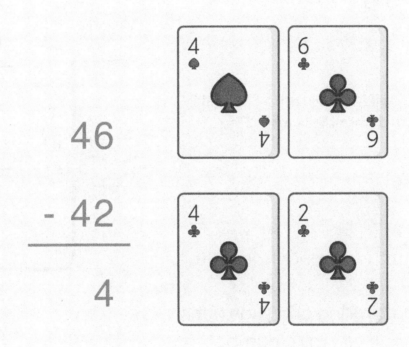

4. The player with the answer closest to zero wins.

999 to zero

PLAYERS: 2-6
SKILL: subtraction, logic
YOU NEED: paper & pencil, dice

1. Give each player a piece of paper.

2. Write 999 at the top of your paper.

3. Choose whether you want to roll 1, 2, or 3 dice on your turn. Make a number with the digits you roll.

   FOR EXAMPLE: If you roll a 6, 3, and 2 you could make the number 632.

```
  999
 -632
  ───
  367
 -214
  ───
  153
```

4. Subtract the number from 999.

5. Take turns rolling and subtracting numbers. If you roll a number that goes below zero, skip your turn.

6. The first player to get to zero **exactly** wins.

multiplication & division games

Lucky Numbers 28

Clippy..29

Just the Facts.......................................30

Two Thousand 31

Factors & Multiples 32

Remainder of Zero 33

2-3-5 34

Super Six 35

Buzz 36

It's Sunday afternoon and you're making 50 cookies for the fund raiser at school tomorrow.

Your kitchen is filled with that delicious, baking cookie smell. It's so yummy and distracting that you keep losing count of how many cookies you've made so far.

Then you notice the cookies are lined up in rows on the cookie sheets.

This reminds you of something your teacher said in class that day: multiplication is a quick way of counting equal groups.

Each row has 5 cookies, and you've baked 6 rows of cookies so far. Multiplication can help you figure out how many more rows you need to bake for the fund raiser!

Multiplication is a shortcut for quickly adding equal groups. Division is a way of sharing equal groups to keep things fair.

Play the games in this chapter to get a taste of what multiplication and division look like in real life.

lucky numbers

PLAYERS: 2
SKILL: multiplication facts
YOU NEED: Hundred Chart, dice, colored markers

1. Print a Hundred Chart as your game board.

2. Roll two dice. Multiply the numbers together.

3. Find the answer on the Hundred Chart. Cross off the number in your color.

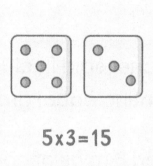

5 x 3 = 15

4. Take turns rolling the dice and crossing off numbers.

5. Use strategy to cross off three numbers in a row—horizontal, vertical, or diagonal.

6. If you roll and get a product that has already been crossed off, you may cross off any available number.

7. The first person to score 3 three-in-a-rows wins.

clippy

PLAYERS: 2
SKILL: multiplication facts
YOU NEED: Clippy Game Board, paper clips, colored markers

1. Print a Clippy Game Board on card stock.

2. Give each player a paper clip and a colored marker.

3. Each player puts a paper clip on one of the numbers at the bottom of the game board.

4. Multiply the two numbers. Cross off the answer with your colored marker.

5. The next player moves ONE of the paper clips, multiplies the two numbers together, and crosses off a different number.

6. The first player to get 4 in a row wins.

42	64	48	15	28
12	14	30	16	25
36	27	63	21	20
54	49	18	✗	56
72	40	45	32	81

2 3 4 5 6 7 8 9

just the facts

PLAYERS: 2-4
SKILL: multiplication facts
YOU NEED: deck of cards

1. Aces are 1, jacks are 11, queens are 12, kings are 100.

2. Decide which set of multiplication facts you want to learn as you play. For example, "Let's do 9's."

3. Find that number in the deck. If you are playing to learn 9's, put the 9 card face up on the table.

4. Put the rest of the deck face down on the table.

5. Each player takes one card from the pile. Do not show your card to the other players.

6. Multiply the number on your card times the number on the table.

Example: You draw a 3.
A 9 is on the table so you say, "I have 27".

7. Each player says their answer out loud.

8. The player with the highest number takes everyone else's cards.

9. The player with the most cards at the end wins.

two thousand

PLAYERS: 2-4
SKILL: multiplication
YOU NEED: paper & pencil, dice

1. Roll a die.

2. Multiply that number times 1, 10, or 100 for your score.

$$6 \times 100 = 600$$

$$2 \times 100 = \underline{200}$$
$$800$$
$$+$$
$$4 \times 100 = \underline{400}$$
$$1200$$
$$+$$
$$6 \times 100 = \underline{600}$$
$$1800$$

3. Take turns rolling and adding to your score each time.

4. The first person to get to 2,000 exactly wins.

factors & multiples

PLAYERS: 2
SKILL: factors and multiples
YOU NEED: Hundred Chart, pencil

1. Print a Hundred Chart as your game board.

2. The first player circles any number under 50 that is not prime.

3. The next player circles a factor or a multiple of that number.

4. Each player finds a factor or a multiple of the last number circled.

5. You cannot re-use a number that has already been circled.

6. Play until there are no more moves to make.

7. The last one to circle a number wins.

level up!

Instead of competing, work together to try and circle as many numbers as you can.

remainder of zero

PLAYERS: 2-3
SKILL: division
YOU NEED: dice

1. Roll 4 dice.

2. Use the digits to make a division problem. The answer must have a remainder of zero.

3. You do not have to use all the numbers you rolled.

4. The answer to the division problem (the quotient) is your score for the round.

EXAMPLE:
You rolled a 5, 1, 3 and a 6.
You made the division problem: 651÷3
The answer is 217. You get 217 points for the round.

5. Play 5 rounds and add up your score.

2-3-5

PLAYERS: 2-4
SKILL: division, divisibility rules
YOU NEED: dice, 2-3-5 Game Board

1. Print out or draw a game board for each player.

2. Roll 2 dice. Use the digits to make a number. (If you roll a 5 and a 1, you could make 51 or 15.)

3. Is your number divisible by 2, 3, or 5? Write your number in one of the columns.

2	3	5
62	36	15
14		

4. If you roll numbers that you cannot play, skip your turn.

5. Take turns rolling and writing in numbers that are divisible by 2, 3, or 5.

6. The first one to fill in their game board wins.

super six

PLAYERS: 2-4
SKILL: division with remainders
YOU NEED: paper & pencil, dice

1. Roll 6 dice (or roll one die 6 times). Add the dots to find your starting number.

4+3+6+2+5+6 = 26 is your starting number

2. All the players use the same starting number (the dividend).

3. Each player rolls a die. This is your divisor; you'll divide the starting number into that many groups. Example: You rolled a 4, so your problem is 26 ÷ 4.

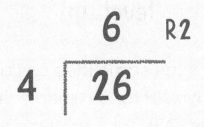

4. Each player solves for the number they rolled.

5. Ignore the remainders. Write the answer (in this case a 6) as your score for the round.

6. Roll 6 dice again for a new starting number.

7. The highest score after 5 rounds wins.

buzz

PLAYERS: 2-6
SKILL: multiples
YOU NEED: no supplies needed

1. This is a counting game. The first person says 1. The second person says 2, and so on.

2. Any time you get to a multiple of 3, say BUZZ instead of the number.

3. Any time you get to a number with a 3 in it, say BUZZ instead of the number.

4. How far can you get without making a mistake?

5. Play with other multiples, like 4 or 9.

level up!

Play Bish Bash Bosh. It's the same idea as Buzz, but a little trickier:
- Say BISH for a multiple of 3
- Say BASH for a multiple of 5
- Say BOSH for a multiple of 3 and 5

fraction & decimal games

Snacktions 40

Copy Cat 41

Fracto Giganto 42

Pizza! 43

The Betting Game 44

Zombies 46

Get in Line 48

Round Four 49

Did you know decimals are sometimes called "decimal fractions"?

Fractions and decimals may look different, but they have similar jobs: they give us a way to talk about **parts and pieces**.

Both fractions and decimals divide things into equal parts. Fractions can divide a whole into any number of parts—like 1/8 (one eighth) of a pizza.

Decimals can only divide a whole into multiples of ten: tenths, hundredths, thousandths, etc.—like 0.1 (one tenth) of a pizza.

Play the games in this chapter to get some hands-on practice for how fractions and decimals work.

snacktions

PLAYERS: 1-4
SKILL: fractions concept
YOU NEED: dice, snacks

1. Put 12 small snacks on a plate for each player.

2. Roll the die. Make a fraction with a 1 on top and your number on the bottom.

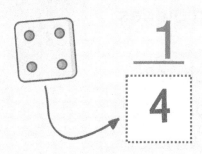

3. If you rolled a 4, you would eat 1/4 of the snacks on your plate.

4. To find 1/4, put your snacks in 4 equal groups. Then eat one of the groups.

5. Add more snacks to make a total of 12 for the next round.

6. If you roll a 5, don't make a fraction. Roll again.

7. Play until you are tired of eating snacks!

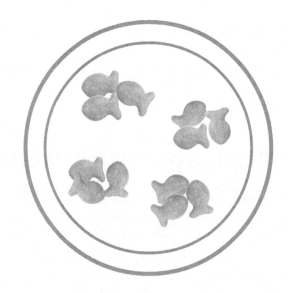

copy cat

PLAYERS: 2
SKILL: comparing fractions
YOU NEED: 4 dice, Fraction Strips

1. Give 2 dice to each player.

2. The first player rolls...and makes...two dice. Make a fraction like this:

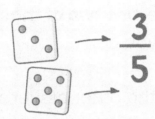

3. The second player copies...either the numerator (top number) or denominator (bottom number) of the other player's fraction.

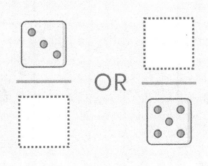

4. Roll your die to fill in the missing number.

5. Compare fractions: which one is bigger? If you're not sure, check your answer with fraction strips.

6. The player with the larger fraction gets $1\frac{1}{2}$ points.

7. Play 8 rounds. The player with the higher score wins.

fracto giganto

PLAYERS: 2
SKILL: comparing fractions
YOU NEED: deck of cards

1. Take out the jacks, queens, and kings. Aces =1

2. Give each player half the deck. Put your cards face down in front of you.

3. Take 4 cards from your pile. Use **two of those cards** to make the largest fraction you can.

4. Compare your fraction to the other player's fraction. Who has the bigger fraction?

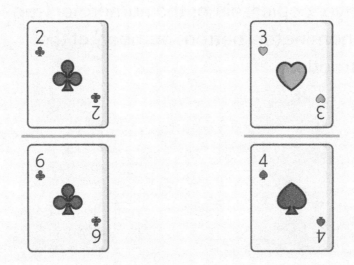

5. The player with the higher fraction takes all 4 cards that were played.

6. Draw another 2 cards, so each of you now have 4 cards to choose from.

7. Play until you can't draw any more cards. The player with the most cards wins.

pizza!

PLAYERS: 2-4
SKILL: adding fractions
YOU NEED: Pizza Game Board, dice

1. Print out the Pizza Game Boards.

2. Roll the die. Color in that many pieces of pizza. If you rolled a 6, you would color 6 pieces of pizza.

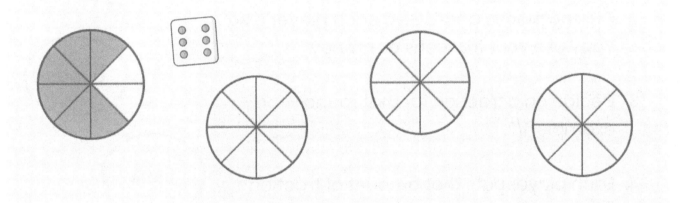

3. The pizzas are cut in eighths. Six pieces of pizza is 6/8 of the pizza.

4. On your next turn, roll for more pieces of pizza.

5. Fill in your score sheet to show how much pizza you have:

Fraction (My Roll)	Total Eighths	Mixed Number
$\frac{6}{8}$	$\frac{6}{8}$	—
$\frac{5}{8}$	$\frac{11}{8}$	$1\frac{3}{8}$

6. The first person to fill in all 4 pizzas wins.

the betting game

PLAYERS: 3-6
SKILL: dividing fractions
YOU NEED: Fraction Strips, dice, one coin

1. Print a set of Fraction Strips for each player on heavy paper or card stock. Make each set a different color to make them easier to sort.

2. Cut the pieces apart. Give each player a set. You'll use your fractions as money.

3. Decide on a fraction for that round--for example, 1/2.

4. Each player puts that amount of fraction strips on the table.

5. Get ready to flip a coin. Each player guesses--heads or tails?

6. Flip a coin. Who guessed correctly?

7. The winners who guessed correctly share the fraction strips fairly between them.

the betting game

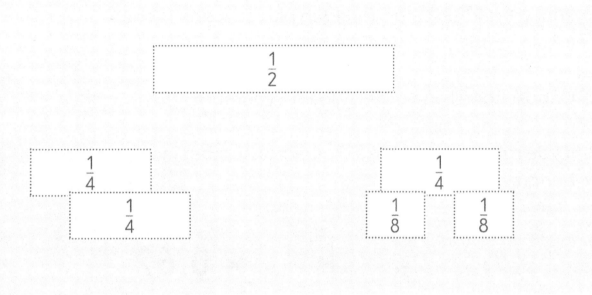

7. You may need to do some trading to share the fraction pieces equally.

8. If a piece is too small to share, leave it on the table to "sweeten the pot" for the next round.

9. Play 8 rounds. Count how much you have in fraction pieces. The player with the highest number wins.

10. Separate your fraction pieces into different envelopes to be ready for the next game.

zombies

PLAYERS: 2
SKILL: decimals concept
YOU NEED: Hundred Chart, dice, colored pencils or markers

1. Print a Hundred Chart for each player. A grid is one whole. This is your game board.

2. Choose to roll one or two dice on your turn.

3. If you roll two dice, make a decimal number in the hundredths.

⚃⚃ ⚂ = 0.62

4. Color in that much of THE OTHER PLAYER'S board. The part you color in shows where the zombies are.

1	2	3	4	5	6	7	8	9	10
11	12	13	14	15	16	17	18	19	20
21	22	23	24	25	26	27	28	29	30
31	32	33	34	35	36	37	38	39	40
41	42	43	44	45	46	47	48	49	50
51	52	53	54	55	56	57	58	59	60
61	62	63	64	65	66	67	68	69	70
71	72	73	74	75	76	77	78	79	80
81	82	83	84	85	86	87	88	89	90
91	92	93	94	95	96	97	98	99	100

zombies

5. If you choose to roll just one die, you must say whether you are rolling for tenths or hundredths BEFORE you roll the die.

 = .05

6. You must roll an exact number to fill in the last of your opponent's board.

7. If you roll a number that you can't play, skip your turn.

8. Once a board is completely filled in, the zombies have invaded!

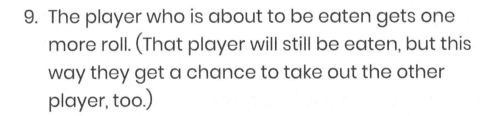

9. The player who is about to be eaten gets one more roll. (That player will still be eaten, but this way they get a chance to take out the other player, too.)

10. Any players still alive at the end of the game win.

get in line

PLAYERS: 2
SKILL: ordering fractions and decimals
YOU NEED: Get In Line Game Board, different-colored markers

1. Print a Get In Line Game Board. Each player takes a different-colored marker.

2. Pick 2 numbers from the list at the bottom of the game board. Make a fraction with the numbers.

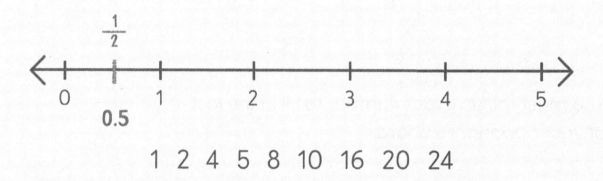

EXAMPLE: You pick a 1 and a 2 and make the fraction 1/2.

3. Write your fraction in the correct spot on the number line in your color.

4. Write the decimal below your fraction.

5. Take turns writing in a new fraction and decimal in your color.

6. The first player to get 4 numbers in a row in their color wins.

round four

PLAYERS: 2
SKILL: rounding decimals
YOU NEED: Round Four Game Board, dice, colored markers

1. Print the game board. Both players will use the same game board.

2. Roll 3 dice.

3. Use the three digits to make a decimal number.

4. For example, you roll 2, 5 and 1. You make the decimal number 21.5 (or 5.12, or some other number).

5. Round it to the nearest whole number.

6. Circle that number on the game board in your color.

7. Take turns making numbers and circling them on the game board.

8. The first player to get 4 in a row wins.

21.5
(or 51.2 or 12.5 etc.)

1	2	3	4	5	6	7
11	12	13	14	15	16	17
21	(22)	23	24	25	26	27
31	32	(33)	34	35	36	37
41	42	43	(44)	45	46	47
51	52	53	54	(55)	56	57
61	62	63	64	65	66	67

level up!

Roll 4 dice and make numbers into the thousandths.

mixed skill games

Bowling for Numbers 52

Flip It 53

Algebra Balance Game 54

Bounce 55

Four Strikes & You're Out 56

Best Bingo Game Ever 58

When you're learning a new math skill, like multiplication, it helps to work on just that one thing for awhile until you get good at it.

But once you know some different math skills, you can get creative and mix things up a little.

In one game, you might add, subtract, multiply, divide, or some combination of all of these.

The games in this chapter will let you get to think differently and try new things.

Each game is different every time, so you can play these over and over again, and it's like a new game each time!

bowling for numbers

PLAYERS: 1
SKILL: addition, subtraction, multiplication, division
YOU NEED: dice, Bowling for Numbers Game Board

1. Print or draw a Bowling for Numbers Game Board.

2. Roll a die 3 times. Write down the three numbers.

3. Use your numbers in any math operation (addition, multiplication, subtraction, division) to total one of the numbers on the game board.

4. Cross off the numbers on the game board as you find them.

5. Let's say you rolled a 2, 6 and a 4.

    ✸ 2 + 6 − 4 = 4 (cross off a 4)

    ✸ 4 − 2 + 6 = 8 (cross off an 8)

    ✸ 6 + 4 = 10 (cross off a 10)

    ✸ 6 x 2 ÷ 4 = 3 (cross off a 3) ...and so on

6. If you can cross off all of the numbers, you get a strike!

7. If you get stuck, roll one more number.

level up!

Use all three numbers in every equation.

flip it

PLAYERS: 1
SKILL: mixed skills
YOU NEED: deck of cards, dice

1. Take an Ace, 2, 3, 4, 5, 6, 7, 8, 9 and 10 from the deck. Aces = 1.

2. Lay out the cards face up on the table, in order from 1-10.

3. Roll 2 dice.

4. Use both numbers with any math operation (addition, subtraction, multiplication or division) to equal one of the numbers on a card.

5. Flip that card over.

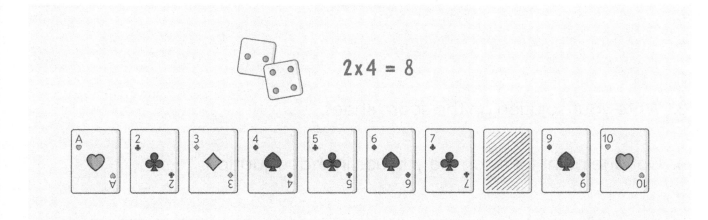

6. If you roll and can't flip a card, you may have a bonus roll to try again. You are allowed no more than 3 bonus rolls per game.

7. Can you flip all your cards over?

algebra balance game

PLAYERS: 2-3
SKILL: mixed skills
YOU NEED: 6 dice, Algebra Balance Score Sheet

1. Print the Algebra Balance score sheet.

2. Roll 6 dice.

3. Use as many of the dice as possible to make an equation that balances. You can use any math operation.

4. All the players work together to find a solution.

$$6 \div (1+2) \qquad = \qquad 5-2-1$$

3. Write your solution on the score sheet.

4. Get one point for each die you use in that equation.

bounce

PLAYERS: 2
SKILL: mixed skills
YOU NEED: paper & pencil

1. Write the numbers 1 to 20.

2. Cross out any two numbers on the number line.

3. Add, subtract, multiply or divide those two numbers to equal a different number on the game board.

4. Circle the answer on the game board.

①　② 　3　4　5　6　~~7~~　8　9　10　11　12　13　~~14~~　15　16　17　18　19　20

$$14 \div 7 = 2$$

5. The next player uses the circled number and one other number to make a math problem.

6. Cross off those two numbers. Circle the answer on the game board.

①　~~②~~ 　3　4　5　6　~~7~~　8　~~9~~　10　11　12　13　~~14~~　15　16　17　⑱　19　20

$$2 \times 9 = 18$$

7. Keep playing, bouncing from one number to another, until you can't make any more moves.

8. The last player to circle a number wins.

four strikes & you're out

PLAYERS: 2-10
SKILL: mixed skills
YOU NEED: paper & pencil

1. Write a math problem with no more than 6 digits. Keep it a secret from the other players.

2. Draw lines to match the digits in your math problem. If your math problem is 23 + 19 = 42, you would write:

_ _ + _ _ = _ _

3. Now you are ready to play. The other players take turns guessing a number from 0-9.

4. Write the number in the spaces that have that digit.

2 _ + _ _ = _ 2

5. When someone guesses a number that is NOT in your math problem, that's a strike.

0 1 2̸ 3 4̸ 5 6 7 8 9

6. If the guessers get 4 strikes, you win the game!

four strikes & you're out

level up!

Try different kinds of math problems. Which ones were the hardest to guess?

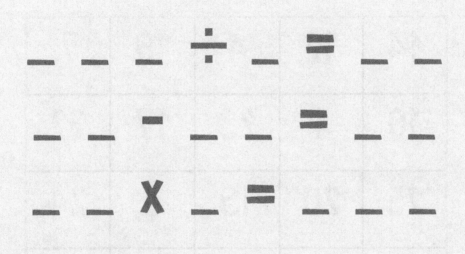

best bingo game ever

PLAYERS: 2-10
SKILL: mixed skills
YOU NEED: Bingo Game Board, dice

1. Print a Bingo Game Board, or draw your own 5x5 grid.

2. Write the numbers 1-25 randomly in the game board.

3. Roll a die 4 times. Write the numbers you rolled below your game board.

14	12	4	19	7
10	1	23	17	22
25	20	15	8	24
3	16	5	2	13
18	11	6	21	9

4   2   1   6

best bingo game ever

4. Use **all four digits** and any math operation (addition, subtraction, multiplication, division) to make a number on the board.

5. You may:

    ❋ Combine digits to make larger numbers   21, 16, 14, 24, etc.

    ❋ Use fractions, square roots, factorials, etc. $6/2 \quad 4^2 \quad \sqrt{4}$

    ❋ Use parentheses $2(4+6) \times 1$

6. You may not:

    ❋ Use a number you did not roll (ex: you cannot make 3^2 if you didn't roll a 2)

7. Work together to make equations and cross off numbers until you get Bingo --or cross off all the numbers for Blackout!

~~14~~	12	4	19	7
10	1	23	17	22
25	~~20~~	15	8	~~24~~
~~3~~	~~16~~	5	2	13
18	11	6	~~21~~	9

printable pages

Hundred Chart 62

Rounding X's Game Board 63

Add 'Em Up Score Card 64

Cross Out Singles Game Board 65

Clear the Deck Game Board 66

Skunk Game Board 67

Penny Nickel Dime Game Board 68

Clippy Game Board 69

2-3-5 Game Board 70

Fraction Strips 71

Pizza Game Board 72

Get In Line Game Board.............................73

Round Four Game Board...........................74

Bowling for Numbers Game Board.........75

Algebra Balance Score Sheet..................76

Bingo Game Board......................................77

Some of the games in this book use special game boards or math tools.

You can copy these from the back of the book, or you can print them online at

    artfulmath.com/miss-brain-extras

hot tip!

Slip your Hundred Chart or game board inside a clear page protector. Write on it with a dry erase marker and you can use it over and over again!

hundred chart

1	2	3	4	5	6	7	8	9	10
11	12	13	14	15	16	17	18	19	20
21	22	23	24	25	26	27	28	29	30
31	32	33	34	35	36	37	38	39	40
41	42	43	44	45	46	47	48	49	50
51	52	53	54	55	56	57	58	59	60
61	62	63	64	65	66	67	68	69	70
71	72	73	74	75	76	77	78	79	80
81	82	83	84	85	86	87	88	89	90
91	92	93	94	95	96	97	98	99	100

rounding x's game board

10	20	30	40	50
60	70	80	90	100

add 'em up score card

score					
	=	=	=	=	=
ones					
	+	+	+	+	+
tens					
	+	+	+	+	+
hundreds					

cross out singles game board

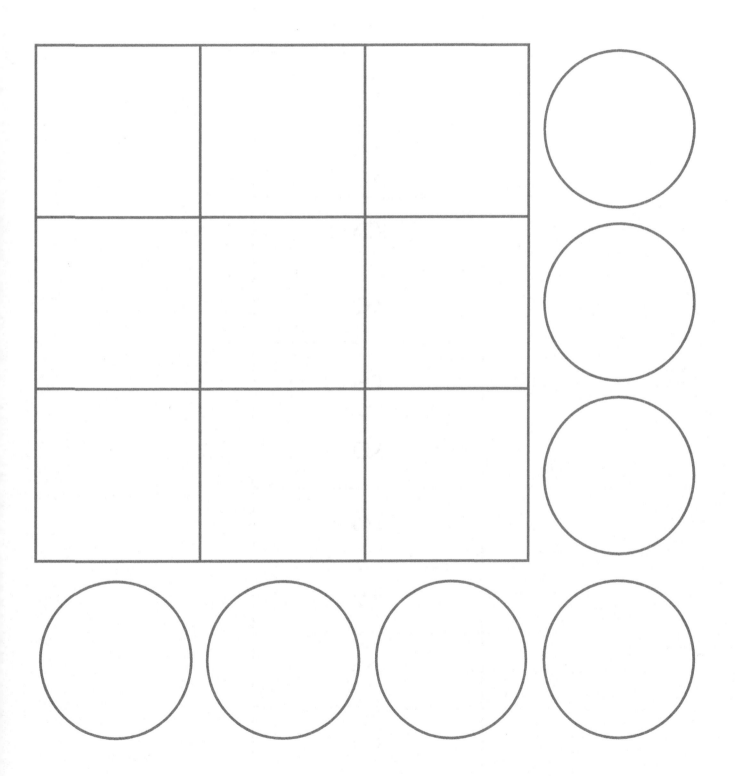

clear the deck game board

12
11
10
9
8
7
6
5
4
3
2

skunk game board

S	
K	
U	
N	
K	

penny nickel dime game board

	Number Rolled	Penny, Nickel or Dime?	Money This Turn	Money So Far
1				
2				
3				
4				
5				
6				
7				

clippy game board

42	64	48	15	28
12	14	30	16	25
36	27	63	21	20
54	49	18	24	56
72	40	45	32	81

2 3 4 5 6 7 8 9

2-3-5 game board

2	3	5

2	3	5

fraction strips

1							
$\frac{1}{3}$		$\frac{1}{3}$			$\frac{1}{3}$		
$\frac{1}{6}$	$\frac{1}{6}$	$\frac{1}{6}$	$\frac{1}{6}$	$\frac{1}{6}$	$\frac{1}{6}$		
$\frac{1}{12}$	$\frac{1}{12}$	$\frac{1}{12}$	$\frac{1}{12}$	$\frac{1}{12}$	$\frac{1}{12}$	$\frac{1}{12}$	$\frac{1}{12}$	$\frac{1}{12}$	$\frac{1}{12}$	$\frac{1}{12}$	$\frac{1}{12}$

1			
$\frac{1}{2}$		$\frac{1}{2}$	
$\frac{1}{4}$	$\frac{1}{4}$	$\frac{1}{4}$	$\frac{1}{4}$
$\frac{1}{8}$	$\frac{1}{8}$	$\frac{1}{8}$	$\frac{1}{8}$	$\frac{1}{8}$	$\frac{1}{8}$	$\frac{1}{8}$	$\frac{1}{8}$

pizza game board

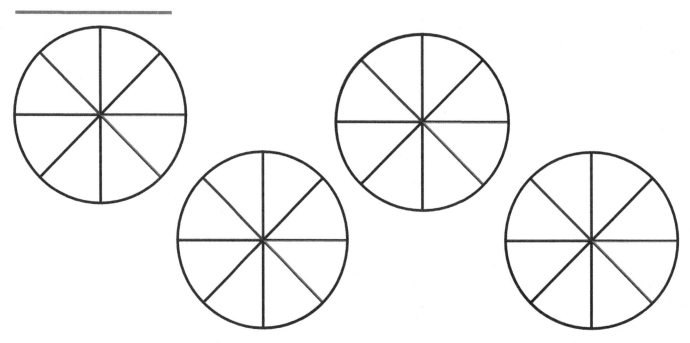

Fraction (My Roll)	Total Eighths	Mixed Number

get in line game board

round four game board

1	2	3	4	5	6	7
11	12	13	14	15	16	17
21	22	23	24	25	26	27
31	32	33	34	35	36	37
41	42	43	44	45	46	47
51	52	53	54	55	56	57
61	62	63	64	65	66	67

bowling for numbers game board

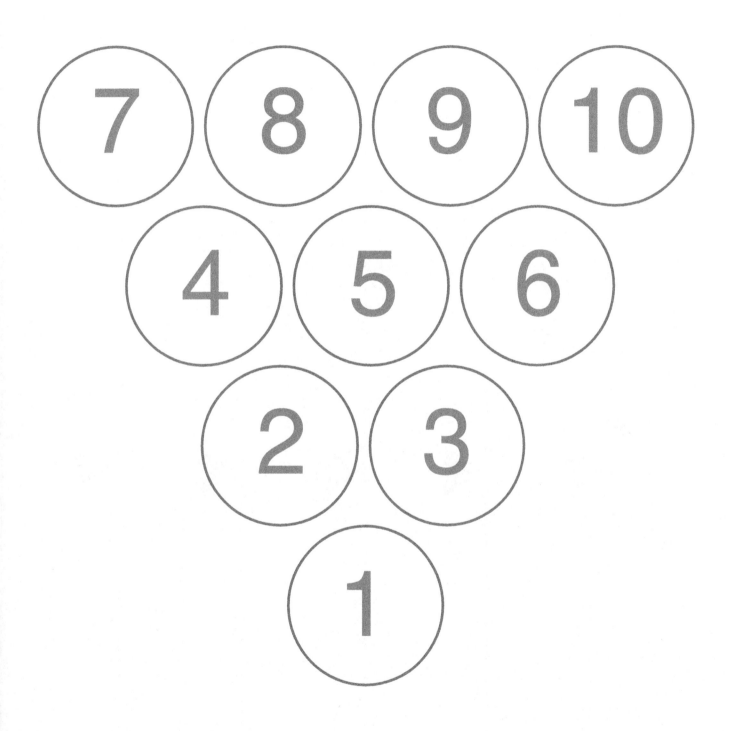

___ ___ ___

algebra balance score sheet

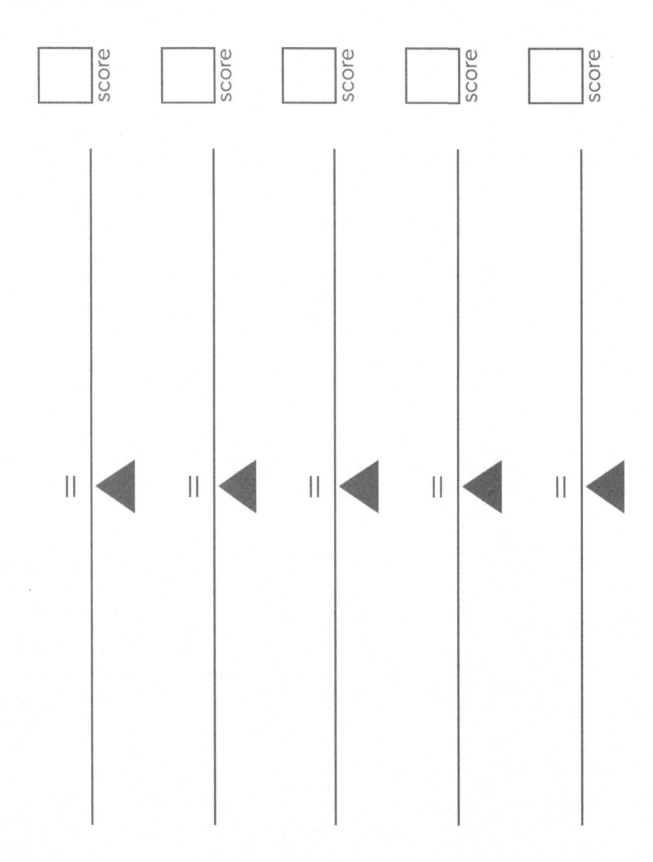

bingo game board

Roll the die 4 times. Write your numbers here.

math dictionary

ALGEBRA
The study of patterns and connections in math.

ARRAY
Arrays are one of the best ways to "see" multiplication. An array is a picture that shows equal groups in rows or columns.

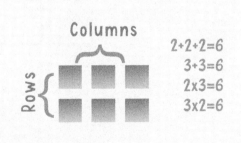

COUNTING ON
The ability to start at any number and keep counting. 34…35, 36, 37.

COUNTERS

Small objects (like beans, buttons, rocks, etc) that you can easily count to solve problems.

DENOMINATOR

The denominator is the bottom number in a fraction. It says how many equal pieces or parts are in one whole.

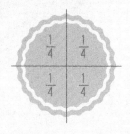

DIE

Two number cubes are called dice; one is called a die.

DIFFERENCE

This is what we call the answer to a subtraction problem. The gap between two numbers is the difference between them.

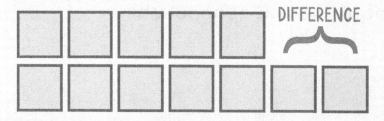

The difference between 7 and 5 is 2.
7-5=2

DIGIT

1 2 3 4 5 6 7 8 9 0
DIGITS

The numbers 0-9 are called digits. Digits can be used together to make bigger numbers. 999 is a 3-digit number.

DIVISIBLE

Divisible means a number can be shared in equal groups with none left over.

12 is divisible by 4

DIVISIBILITY RULE

A trick that helps you quickly know if a number is divisible by another number. For example, a number that is divisible by 5 will always end in a 5 or a 0.

EVEN NUMBER

Even numbers show quantities that can be paired up evenly; each one has "a friend". Even numbers always end in 0, 2, 4, 6, or 8.

Six is an even number.
Each one has "a friend."

EQUAL

The amount on both sides of the equal sign balance each other out. Each side has the same total.

$2 \times 3 = 7 - 1$

EQUATION

A math problem where the amount on both sides of the equal sign is the same.

$6 \times 10 = 60$
$9 = 4 + 5$
$12 - 4 = 5 + 3$

FRACTION

We use fractions to talk about something that has been divided into equal-sized parts. 2/3 of a pizza means you have 2 of the 3 pieces.

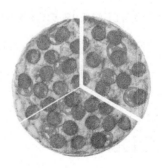

HUNDRED CHART

A chart with numbers from 1 to 100. It makes it easy to see patterns and connections between numbers.

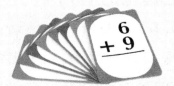

MATH FACTS

Basic math problems like 3+2 and 2x5 are called math facts.

NUMERATOR

The top number of a fraction. It tells us how many pieces or parts we're talking about.

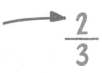

ODD NUMBER

When you put objects in pairs and there is an extra one left over, the number is odd. Odd numbers end in 1, 3, 5, 7 or 9.

Seven is an odd number. When each dot is paired up with a friend, one dot is left out on its own.

PLACE VALUE

Place value is our system for how numbers work. The number 5 means 50 if it's moved to the tens place, or 500 in the hundreds place.

PRODUCT

The answer to a multiplication problem.

QUOTIENT

The answer to a division problem.

REGROUPING

Regrouping is the process of making and sharing groups of ten to solve a problem. It is also known as borrowing and carrying.

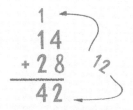

ROUNDING

When you don't need an exact answer, you can use a number close by that ends in zero. Rounding to a "friendly number" makes a math problem easier to solve.

37 rounds to 40

SKIP COUNTING

If we count by 5s to 100, we skip over all the numbers that are not multiples of 5. Skip counting is a fast way of counting that is a first step in learning multiplication.

5, 10, 15, 20…

SUM

The answer to an addition problem.

you might also like...

Kitten Math

Enter into an imaginary world of fostering tiny, 3-week-old kittens...and learn math as you care for your fuzzy babies.

It truly is the most adorable math project ever!

Nature Math

What would you say if I told you there's a secret pattern hidden in nature—in plants & flowers, snail shells, and even your own body?

Discover math through art and the outdoors in this amazing, real-world workbook.

Get your copies of Kitten Math and Nature Math at <u>amazon.com</u>.

take the quiz

Did you know, your brain has its own best way to learn math?

- Some kids learn best by playing games.

- Others like math that is a natural part of real-world experiences.

- Kids who are visual thinkers may like to learn math by drawing pictures.

When a person tries to learn in a way that doesn't work for their brain, they might think they're bad at math.

Do you think you're bad at math? If so your brain just needs to learn math a different way.

Discover your math superpower, and find out how YOUR brain learns math best!

Take the quiz today at:

artfulmath.com/superpower-quiz

index

2-3-5	34
999 to Zero	24
Add 'Em Up	12
Algebra Balance Game	54
Best Bingo Game Ever	58
The Betting Game	44
Bounce	55
Bowling for Numbers	52
Buzz	36
Clear the Deck	17
Clippy	29
Close to Zero	23
Copy Cat	41
Cross Out Singles	16
Fracto Giganto	42
Factors & Multiples	32
Farkle Junior	22
Flip It	53
Four Strikes & You're Out	56
Garbage Dump	9
Get in Line	48
Just the Facts	30
Likeable Numbers	8
Lucky Numbers	28
Ninety Nine	20
Numbaroll	6
Penny Nickel Dime	19
Pizza!	43
Remainder of Zero	33
Round Four	49
Rounding X's	11
Secret Number	10
Skunk	18
Snacktions	40
Sneaky 15	7
Super Six	35
Two Thousand	31
Zombies	46

Made in the USA
Las Vegas, NV
20 December 2024